Shapes, colours and matching, too,
Learning with Barney is fun to do!

£5.99

Contents

Creative Director	Tricia Legault	Contributing Illustrators	Darren McKee
Editorial Director	Guy Davis		Becky Winslow
Editor	Gayla Amaral		Jay Johnson
			Darrell Baker
			Chris Sharp
			Gary Currant
		Designer	Whitney G. Center

Published by
GRANDREAMS LIMITED
435-437 Edgware Road, Little Venice
London W2 1TH

Barney's Amazing Alphabet Maze

Barney is trying to find all the letters in the alphabet – from A to Z.

Can you help Barney find objects that begin with each letter as you travel along the alphabet maze? Find an Apple 🍎 that begins with A, then a Ball ⚾ that begins with B, and keep going until you reach the letter Z. When you reach the end, sing the "Alphabet Song".

Silly Alphabet Soup!

Yummy! Chef Barney is making alphabet soup, but some of his ingredients are silly.

Match each letter to the food that begins with that letter to help Barney make the soup.
Which other foods would be silly to put in soup?

Aa

Bb

Cc

9

Barney's™ Book of Shapes

by Mark S. Bernthal

While walking in
the park one day,
Barney spies
some shapes
at play.

"They are playing
many games!
Would you like
to learn
their names?"

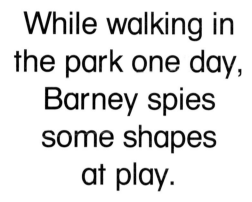

Cecil the **Circle** is round like a ball.

That's his favourite toy of all!

Circle

Sidney the **Square** has four sides the same size.

He likes to picnic and eat cherry pies!

Square

Theresa the **Triangle** has three sides.

She zooms down the playground slide!

Triangle

Rosie the **Rectangle** has four sides. She likes to go on pony rides.

With two sides short and two sides long, Rosie sings a happy song.

Rectangle

Orville the **Oval** looks like an egg.

He likes to toss horseshoes over a peg!

Oval

Debbie the **Diamond** is shaped like her kite…

…flying high in the sky past clouds that are white!

Diamond

There are
five points on
Steven the **Star**.

He's very proud
of his shiny
red car!

Star

While taking a walk, Hilary the *Heart*...

...is pulling four puppies in her blue cart!

Heart

Star

Diamond

Oval

Circle

28

Heart

Rectangle

Triangle

Square

When playing with shapes, the fun never ends. Can you name all of Barney's new friends?

Ringmaster Barney is having fun under
the Big Top! There are lots of hidden shapes at
Barney's Imagination Circus.

CIRCUS SHAPES

Can you find these shapes?
Square ☐, Circle ⬤, Triangle ▲, Rectangle ▮,
Diamond ◆, Heart ♥, Oval ⬮ and Star ☆.

Matching Game

Baby Bop is playing in her garden.

Can you help her match the things that look alike?

Colour Fun!

Barney, Baby Bop and BJ have a fun day learning about colours.

Can you find the objects below that match these colours?

Green   Blue   Yellow   Red

35

Fun With Opposites!

Barney wants you to play a game with opposites. Point to a picture of Barney and then find the picture that shows the opposite.

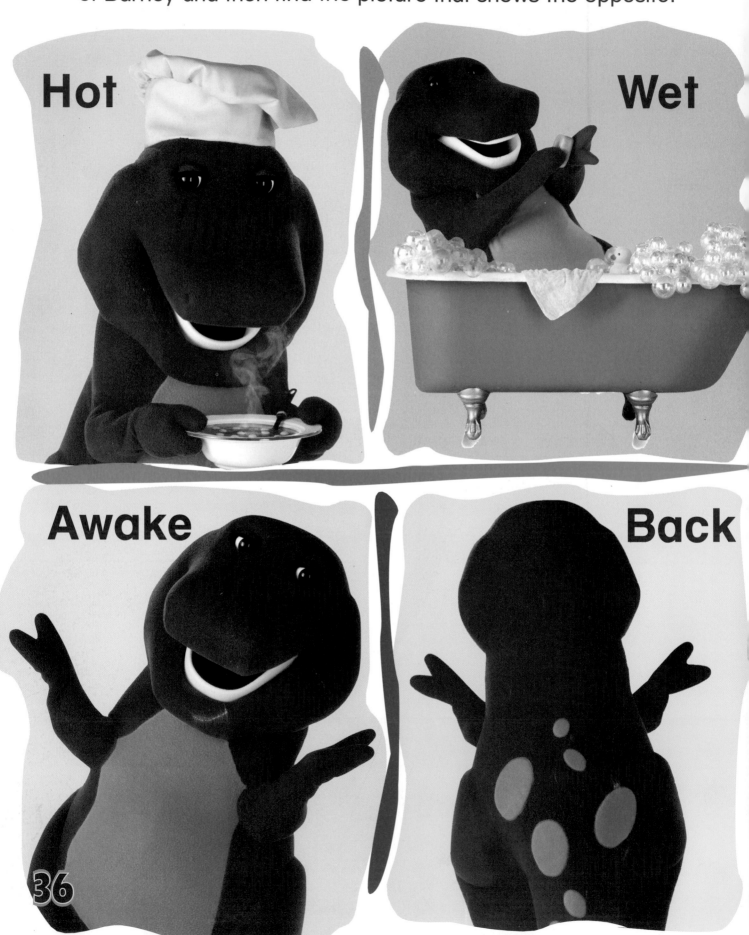

Hot

Wet

Awake

Back

Here's a clue to get you started. Barney's soup is hot.
Can you find something that is the opposite of hot?

Asleep   Front

Dry   Cold

37

Barney's Time for Counting

by Sandy Payne

"Look what time it is!" says Barney to Baby Bop. "It's time for counting!"

Barney has **1** alarm clock.
Baby Bop has **1** blankey.

"I'm wearing my new sunglasses," says Barney.

40

"We have 1, **2** sunglasses for a sunny day," says Baby Bop.

"Barney, look! I see **3** flowers!"
exclaims Baby Bop.

42

Baby Bop sees 1, 2, **3** flowers.

"I like apples,"
giggles Baby Bop.

4

"Listen!" Barney whispers. "I hear **5** birds singing!"

"1, 2, 3, 4, **5** pretty birds,"
counts Baby Bop.

5

"There are **6** clouds in the sky," Barney says.
"I think it might rain!"

"I'm glad we have our umbrellas," says Baby Bop.

6

"It's raining!" Barney says.

"I see **7** ducks playing in the rain!"
says Baby Bop.

7

"Barney, will you read a story to me?"
Baby Bop asks.
"I'd love to," says Barney.

Baby Bop and Barney have **8** books.

"What should we do now?" Baby Bop asks Barney.

54

"Let's play dress-up with these **9** hats!" says Barney.

"Can we colour now?" asks Baby Bop.
"I love to colour!"

"I like to colour, too," agrees Barney. "Look! I see **10** crayons."

"Rain or shine – counting is fun!"
Barney says.

1 2 3 4
5 6 7 8
9 10

Barne

60

Toy Factory

Well done!
You made it!

Baby Bop and BJ visit a terrific toy factory, but they can't find Barney. Can you help them find Barney?

As you move through the maze of toys, try to find these things: